Musings from an Extroverted Introvert

Summer Ward

BookLeaf Publishing

Summer Ward

Presentation by *BookLeaf Publishing*

Web: www.bookleafpub.com

E-mail: info@bookleafpub.com

ISBN: 978-93-5721-353-0

First edition 2023

This book is for Chloe Grace, the love of my life. Watching you move through the world with passion and wonder makes everyday worth living, and I am so proud to be your mom.

ACKNOWLEDGEMENT

To the people that I have met on adventures, both near and far, this book exists because of you.

The Caterpillar

I began truly exploring the idea of who I am during an experience in 8th grade when I auditioned for the play *Alice in Wonderland*. Everyone remembers the psychedelic and impatient caterpillar that the protagonist encounters after falling down the rabbit hole.

As the director was clearly scouring the crowd for who could play such an eccentric role, she landed on my face and called me up. I faked the long cigarette (or whatever he might have been ingesting at that time), and calmly placed my body into the position I inherently knew this character would take.

“WHOOOOO AAAAARRREEEE YOOOOUUUU?”

The first line of this scene escaped my mouth with such fervor and conviction that I knew the part was mine before I even concluded the dialogue with my stage partner.
I spent the next six weeks preparing for a role that would only allow me approximately twelve minutes of stage time.

But isn't that the perfect metaphor?

Being cast as what felt like a tiny part.

A part that needed someone to portray it with the exact right amount of gusto and passion.

A part whose most well-known line is imploring one to answer the question, "Who are you?"

A caterpillar.
The waiting.
The listening.
The learning.
The introspection.
The growth.
The change.

Sometimes, the tiny parts are designed to teach you the most.

Every caterpillar must go through a transformation.
Some phases are more enjoyable than others, but they are all necessary to turn you into the beautiful butterfly the world knows only you can be.

WHISPERS

The Universe kept throwing things at me
That I could no longer ignore.
Actually,
Propelling is a better word.
Better yet,
Catapulting.

She was catapulting things in my direction
with all of Her might.
The first hints seemed to come in whispers;
A word here,
A song lyric there.
Then,
After Mother Earth realized
That I just couldn't seem to grasp a clue,
the hints started to come in a normal speaking
voice;
A quote given directly to me from a close friend.
A situation that one of my students may be
experiencing
That parallels a lesson that I need to learn as
well.
When THAT didn't seem to do the trick,
she started to scream at me.
An injured knee to slow me down.
Bronchitis to stop me in my tracks.

Nightly wake ups between 3 and 5am.

Do you know what waking up between 3 and 5am suggests?
Let me refer you to an article that the Universe kindly tossed my way when I began to realize it was time to start digging deeper.
Paraphrased:
Waking up between 3 and 5 is associated with an energy connected to sadness.
This sadness is quiet and unexplained,
But often relates to the true calling of our heart and soul.
Sitting with that stillness and sadness is the only way
To sift through and truly understand its purpose.
And with this information,
The Universe knew she had finally gotten through.
And I began to write.

Finding Your Why

What is your WHY?
I mean what is your chocolate?
That delectable thing that you crave in life?
What sets your soul on fire and puts air in your lungs?
Some people never find it,
Some are lucky to stumble upon it in the middle of the search,
And others don't even know where to begin.
I think asking yourself what your answer is
is exactly the place to begin;
Everyone needs a starting point,
and the simple realization that this MUST be found is the first step on your journey.
And that is exactly what it is:
A journey.
An adventure.
There is no better time to begin than today.

Although this may be a question I start throwing in everyone's direction,
I think it is also a journey of self discovery.
What is MY why?
What are my Reese's Pieces?
I feel like my board game of life has a START square,

And then branches off into a hundred directions--
Every path full of promise,
Both joy and pain along each road.
You simply can't fully enjoy the epic view from a mountaintop
Until you have been down to the bottom of the valley.
I have spent time in both places,
And feel certain that you need both experiences.
It's called balance.
Even when you are in the pit of despair, feeling utterly alone
And like nobody would understand,
THAT is the moment you chime into what a royally ridiculous thought that is.
You mean to tell me that in ALL of human existence,
You are completely alone in whatever you are feeling?
False.
Breathe in that pain,
Regret,
Wounded pride,
(You fill in the blank),
And then exhale.
Send light and love to all of the people past, present, and future

Who are experiencing the same lesson that you are.
And THAT is exactly what the valley is--
A lesson.
Now ask yourself why?
What is this experience here going to teach me?
In the same way, be thankful when you reach that peak!
Breathe it in,
Smile,
And exhale slowly.
You never know how long it will last.
Think back to the hike that brought you there.
Was it an easy walk at times,
Then a trek where a pole is required to help you jump over dangerous rocks and bumps along the way?
You worked hard to get there.
ENJOY THE HELL OUT OF IT.
Now, thinking through all of it,
The good,
The bad,
And the ugly…
What was your Why?
What brought you to the top?
What did you see?
Experience?
THAT is what makes you tick.
Strive for that every day of your life.

Fight hard for it, no matter what part of the
journey you are on.
A day in the park,
Or in the trenches of the battleground,
Set your eyes on the prize.
You deserve nothing less than that feeling,
and the deep sigh of relief that comes with truly
knowing who you are
And what makes you tick.
Now that you know yourself a little better,
And hopefully you like yourself,
Take care of you FIERCELY
With every ounce of your being.
You
are
worth
it.

Teaching

I believe that teaching is the highest calling one can have.
I have worked with kindergarten and first grade students after school in College Station.
I have taught kindergarten in Tahoe City, California.
I have taught fifth and sixth grade language arts and social studies in Grand Prairie.
I have taught sixth, seventh, and eighth grade language arts in Flower Mound.
I have taught sixth grade science in Bedford.
And finally, I have taught and am currently teaching high school English in Coppell.

I can attest to the fact that it does not matter
Which city you are in,
Level you are at,
Or the subject you are teaching.
What matters is how you
treat
those
kids
in
your
room.

Showing up every single day,
And living a completely authentic version of yourself
Is what those kids need more than anything.
That engaging mitosis lesson you spent six hours creating?
That interactive fraction activity you spent days on?
Those may be forgotten in weeks,
But the way you smiled as they walked in the door,
Or the comfortable classroom you provided on a daily basis
Will be what they remember forever.
We are so much more than our title;
Teacher can also mean being a school mom,
Fellow learner,
Therapist,
Tyer of shoes,
Wiper of tears,
And keeper of silly secrets.
It can mean mentor,
Master of math skills,
Fellow sports enthusiast,
Friendly face between classes,
Or a positive comment at the end of a long day.
We are simply some adults in their lives that they know they can count on.

These kids come to us in all shapes and sizes.
Some ate a pancake feast for breakfast,
While others may not even have a table at home to eat on.
Some have the newest pair of Jordans,
While others can't even find a shirt that fits in their closet.
I have had students act up in class,
And when I ask them to step into the hall with Me so I can see if they are okay,
They break down and tell me their mom hasn't been home in days.
Or that they are so hungry, they can't think.
We have to meet our students
where
they
are.
We have to get to know each and every one of them and cultivate an environment where they feel love and belonging
every
single
day.

The hours are long, some days challenge you to your very core,
But it is absolutely worth it.
That lightbulb finally switching on after days of tutoring.

That first word out of a learner's mouth that has refused to interact.
That smile after tears have flowed from their eyes because you truly listened to them.
Put down your phone.
Put down the pen you are ferociously grading with.
Look into their eyes and listen.
Isn't that what we all want in life?
To be acknowledged, truly heard, and deeply loved?
Try it,
You could change a life.

Regret

I lost it on you last night. Like completely blew
my fuse. It is 3:27 in the morning and I am filled
with sorrow and regret.
I am literally sobbing silently at the kitchen table
as I type this because I need to remember how
this feels.
How I feel.
How I made you feel.
And vow to us both to never do that again.
I am so incredibly tired.
Being your mom is the honor and privilege of
my life, but sometimes it gets really heavy.
I feel like I have poured and poured into you the
past 17 days that we have been together, and you
have poured into me. We have not been more
than a maximum of 16 stairs away this entire
time.
You just wanted me to lay down with you.
You just wanted to understand why we couldn't
sleep together.
You just wanted to be next to me,
And I broke.
I needed space.
I needed a few minutes to just be Summer
Instead of mommy, but I should have just
Enjoyed a sleep story and snuggled with you.

Instead, I yelled.
I exploded.
You depend on me to be your rock and foundation, and most of the time I can be that, but for some reason
I
couldn't
last
night.
I went into your room to snuggle with you in bed and tell you I love you at about 4.
You were completely out.
I came back to my bed and cried a bit more before succumbing to sleep.
I woke up at 6:31 to you in front of me wanting to get in bed and snuggle.
I pulled you in, told you, "I love you and I am so so sorry."
You said the same and hugged me tighter.
The
world
was
at
peace
again.

THE PARK

Do you remember getting home from school and
immediately asking to go to the park?
Do you remember the excitement as you waited
for your teacher to announce it was time for
recess?
On the perfect sunny day.
Not a cloud in sight.
Seventy degrees
With a cool breeze
Flowing through the trees.
Do you remember gleefully flying down a slide
at your local playground?
Can you picture that slide in your mind right
now?
What color is it?
What shape?
How does it curve?
Are your friends in line behind you,
Waiting for you at the bottom?
Have you done that after the age of 8?
Have you done that as a teen?
Twenties?
Thirties?
When I was in high school, my friends and I
would often go to the park and swing.

I lived in a neighborhood just across from a duck pond.
Of course the geese had to be avoided,
But the rest of the backdrop served as a serene scene after a long day.
Boyfriend broke up with a friend?
Park.
Took a test you studied hours for, only to fail miserably?
Park.
I had many first kisses at that park.
I even got engaged to the father of my child right next to my favorite bench on one end of that pond.
In college, I made sure to find the closest park to fulfill this need.
We often went to swing after the same occasions.
New friends, new environment, same outlet.
A quick slide down, and you were a new person.
While sliding…
Can anyone be sad?
Can anyone be angry?
Can anyone be disappointed?
While swinging…
Can anyone be sad?
Can anyone be angry?
Can anyone be disappointed?
Even if only for two point four seconds,

the world feels lighter as you
f r e e f a l l.
Your task for today:
Go find a park with a slide.
Park your car and climb to the top.
Go by yourself or rope someone into the outing with you.
You will not regret it.

Huckleberry Finn

I got my dog from a stripper on Craigslist ten years ago.
True story.
The first picture I saw was him sitting in the snow.
He was 4 months old,
He had black and white fur,
Mixing to make the perfect replica of a tuxedo that he lived in.
I quickly decided that was him.
After some correspondence back and forth,
We decided to meet at Best Buy.
I got out of my car,
She got out of hers and opened the back door of a suburban.
There he was.
He was flattened out like a pancake,
All four of his legs were as straight as could be to give him the ability to be as close to the floor as possible.
I gave her the money,
And she shrugged and said,
"He doesn't like car rides. Good luck!"
I picked him up like a big baby
And he rode in the car like that the whole way home.

Sitting in my lap,
One arm around each side of my neck,
One leg on each side of my waist.
I knew on that first car ride, with the shaking bundle of fur and nerves in my lap, that he would be the best dog I could ever have.
He rode like that everywhere we went for an entire year.
As he gained confidence, he became my co-pilot.
He would sit in the passenger seat
With a big smile plastered across his face everywhere we went.
I originally chose his name because I knew within those first few minutes of meeting him that we would go on countless adventures together,
Just like Twain's character.
I got pregnant after a few years, and he was by my side the entire time.
Once my belly started to grow, he would keep his head on her.
I comfort him when he has bad dreams and he does the same for me.
He comforted me as we were snuggled in a closet
before,
during,
and after my divorce.

He absolutely hates water,
Yet willingly came into the ocean after me.
He always runs as far away as possible to poop and when he can't walk back
Because we are surprised with a snowstorm,
He looks pitifully at me as his limbs betray him and refuse to move.
I go into mom mode and run to him before carrying him through the frozen tundra back to safety;
He holds onto me like he did the first day I met him--
Arms around my neck,
Legs around my waist.
Love this pure is hard to find,
And I am so thankful for that stripper on Craigslist that decided he wasn't for her.
Because he was for me.
And I was for him.

My First Race

I started running one afternoon in college
When I was angry at my boyfriend
And needed to get away for a bit.
Instead of retail therapy,
Which was actually just window shopping
As university students have no money to spend
on unnecessary shenanigans,
I put on my only pair of running shoes and
headed out.
We lived in an apartment off campus,
So I hit the main road, and found the nearest
sidewalk.
With nothing in tow but my iPod nano circa
2006,
I began the first official run of my life.
I
felt
free.
I ran for about half an hour before heading back
home.
My body felt better.
My head felt better.
My heart felt better.
My soul felt better.
It was as if I had just unlocked this new realm
that had the potential to change my life.

I liked the feeling so much that I started looking around for races.
Most people sign up for a 5K when first starting out…
Not me.
In typical Summer style,
I found a half marathon taking place down the street a few months away
And signed up.
I went from running one mile in eighth grade on the very first day of school--
The one and only day I was ever into athletics in my entire life
Before QUITTING because one mile was far too much,
To running 13.1 miles.
PAYING to run 13.1 miles.
How does one prepare to run a half marathon?
Running.
Did I have any knowledge of how to get my body ready?
Nope.
I began going to the university gym most afternoons,
Or running the route I did that first day.
Then I began to branch out and try new sidewalks.
My body began to change.
My head began to change.

My heart began to change.
My soul felt awake and
I
LOVED
IT.
Fast forward to the race morning.
I had trained at the gym or on beautiful, sunny days.
Race day consisted of 30 degree weather,
Paired with 20 mile an hour wind.
To put it lightly,
I WAS MISERABLE.
I WAS UNPREPARED.
I WAS IN HELL.
The hills continued to roll,
And my feet continued to throb.
Mile marker eight loomed in front of me as thoughts of inadequacy filled my head.
Why did I sign up for this?
Crying with snot flying out of both nostrils,
I finally reached the finish line.
I got to my car and gave myself a pep talk.
I had done this really hard thing.
Eighth grade Summer would never believe this could happen!
I ran this race for her,
And for me.
And though I truly thought I would never partake in another race,

I have now conquered 57 half marathons, and four full marathons.
How about that, eighth grade Summer?

WADDLEFEST 2019

My mom and I took Chloe to one of the biggest furniture stores around.
When I say biggest,
I mean the street it's on is named after the establishment,
And I could easily spend the better part of a week meandering from one section to the next.
Our goal was to find Chloe a bed,
And the amount of options was overwhelming to this 31 year old,
So I tried to put myself in my almost 5 year old's shoes.
It was as if I had asked the question aloud,
And her answer was clear.
She was running back and forth between each potential bed,
Much like a pinball flies from one bumper to the next.

It was around bed number seventeen that she hit her shin against a piece of wood.
Even though the damage was a centimeter wide surface scratch producing zero blood,
She was "no longer able to walk."
That is putting it lightly.
My drama queen was now following us around,

dragging her right foot along the ground
exclaiming to anyone in earshot that she
couldn't walk.
Her face was scrunched up as much as the skin
would allow,
And tears were streaming down her face as she
hobbled along,
And I finally took pity.
I picked her up and the tears instantly vanished!
She was smiling and laughing until I had to put
her down again.
Round two of Waddlefest 2019.
I picked her up again until she spotted
something the universe was calling her to
explore.
"Mommy! Put me down!"
And wouldn't you know it, that child could
SPRINT.
My little Forrest Gump was back in action
because she had seen a kitchen set out of the
corner of her teary eye.
I shook my head and laughed,
Because I expect nothing less from the fun
loving, joyful spirit I have the pleasure of calling
my daughter.

It didn't hit me until the next morning as we
were driving,
Singing, and dancing (you know, the usual)

on our way to grandma's for a playdate.
Isn't that how we all are?
We may not literally be leaping from bed to bed at a furniture store before getting wounded,
But issues tend to happen just as quickly and abruptly.
We go about life with a smile,
Whether real or fake,
Until something knocks us down.
Depending on how big or small of a problem determines how long we hobble around
And take part in our own waddlefest.
The woe is me mentality lasts until we see our next ray of sunshine,
Be it a kitchen set around the corner,
Or a kind word from a colleague.
I know I am definitely at fault for this more times than I would like to admit,
But now I am going to challenge myself to avoid the waddlefests when they want to take over.

Life is sometimes brutal,
And you may feel like the hobbling has become a permanent part of your being,
But go find your kitchen set!
Keep going.
You never know,
It could be waiting for you just around the corner.

GOOD STUFF CHEAP

The older I get,
The more I realize how important it is to be around
And get to know my parents as people.
Huck and I arrived this afternoon
With smiles and a short agenda.
I needed to give him a bath,
And then we could enjoy couch time for a few hours before returning home.

After the bath,
I ended up enjoying an unexpected journey--
Ollie's with my mom and dad.
We wandered up and down aisles of books,
And each one of us ended up perusing the store with our selected novel.
My dad rarely goes to any stores
And I should have just followed him around,
And recorded the comments that came out of his mouth
Throughout the duration of our outing.
My favorite
(that I actually got to hear,
who knows how many other jewels left that man's mouth without me in earshot),
"This stuff is too cheap not to buy it all!"

I would argue with any of Ollie's CEO, COO, or other high up position that this should actually be the tagline for the store.
What is actually displayed under the name of every store reads,
"Good Stuff Cheap".
Despite the fact that this is not even proper English,
I think my dad's words would sell more self proclaimed
"Good stuff" for the company.
Clearly, I need to talk my dad into going out more.

HaLF #52

In September of 2021,
I ran my 52nd half marathon.
I woke up feeling like complete garbage
And hit the alarm clock at least 4 times.
I ate some macaroni as I took Huck out,
And then I hit the road.
After a 45 minute drive,
I parked and proceeded to put mascara on.
Wandering through the Dallas Arboretum,
I decided to follow some people that were at least pretending to know where they were headed before we found the starting line.
I put on my music and took a few deep breaths.
A world with Rona has put a damper on in person races over the past two years,
And this would be my second in person half in the calendar year.
I have made it a habit of choosing one person to dedicate my race to,
And one thing to focus on as each mile marker goes by.
While walking to the starting line,
I chose my dad,
But as things started moving,
I decided to focus on finding joy inside of yourself

With many people in mind.
My personal focus was about being present.
Sometimes I choose breathing,
Others I choose form,
But those didn't feel adequate for what the universe has been teaching me lately.

After dropping Chloe off at school three days prior,
I decided the weather was forgiving enough to walk around the pond
At The Sound for a bit before crossing the busy street and going to work.
I was listening to a podcast
And looking around at nature.
Things I had seen thousands of times were new.
I watched ducks waddle by in small groups
And promptly declared their walk to be my favorite of all the animals on earth.
The little squatty bodies,
And tails that awkwardly move from side to side
As they put one foot in front of the other.
I could have watched them wander around for hours.
Then I spotted a white crane positioned
in the corner of the lake,
In the perfect position to overlook the entire scene.

I have gone back and forth for years trying to decide on a mantra,
And it suddenly came to me.
Calm as a crane.
Done.
That's it.
I meandered back to my car,
Deep in thought,
Before walking into my classroom to prepare for the day.
That mental picture of ducks with a single crane watching over
Has played in my mind on loop since then.
Being present during the race
Meant reciting my new mantra numerous times throughout the thirteen miles in my head.
The weather was perfect for the first five miles,
And it was easy to stay calm and present.
Then, the sun came out in full force
And the heat radiated onto my skin.
I mentally maneuvered back to the idea of finding internal joy
For the people in my life.
I started with my dad,
Then mom,
Then Chloe,
Then sister,
And then I realized that I too, need to find that for myself.

What brings me internal joy?
Not from an outside source,
But intrinsically.
While deep in thought,
I started to notice that I would adopt the pace of whoever was around me at various points in the race.
Although my competitive side wanted to at least place in my age group,
I decided that the only person I needed to be competing against
Was myself.
Suddenly, the number seven popped into my head.
I wanted to be seven minutes faster than I was the last time
I ran this course three years ago.
Seemed random but potentially manageable
If I would stop focusing on the speed of others and check in with my pace on my Garmin instead.
Then of course the English teacher in me took over,
And saw this as an analogy for life:

Stop adopting the pace,
Work ethic,
Mentality,
Mood,

Etc of the people around you.
You need to strive to be the best YOU
Instead of checking in with others
And re-evaluating your own needs and wants.
This is also why it is vital to surround yourself with people who are also striving to do and be better.
I quickly started passing people after this realization,
And ended up winning second in my age group.
And my time?
Exactly seven minutes faster…
to
the
second.
I was amazed,
But I also knew that it was a snuggle from the universe.
Stop focusing on others around you for validation
Or asking them for maps that show you which direction your life needs to take.
Be present.
Be better than who you were yesterday.
And always remember to be
calm as a crane.

Miami

Today we embark on our first trip
COMPLETELY alone!
Packing with you for this adventure was
immediately one of my favorite memories
As I could feel the excitement oozing from your
voice
With each piece of clothing you chose to put in
the suitcase.
Not only that,
But you already proved to be a pro as you rolled
each and every item
Before carefully deciding on the proper Tetris
position.
I set the alarm early so I could snag a run.
I wasn't going to be able to log any miles over
the next three days
So this was vital.
Instead of being able to go downstairs
And jump on the treadmill uninterrupted,
You popped up and started talking to me after
the alarm.
I should have known better.
I create a beautifully cultivated plate
Of cinnamon rolls and donut holes
For you to have breakfast in bed with Huck,
and head downstairs.

Grandma shows up at the one mile mark,
And she jumps in bed to enjoy snuggle time with you.
I complete 6 miles and jump in the shower.
You interrupt me a minimum of 4 times,
But what else is new?
I check everything off of my "morning of" list (yes, I am still borderline OCD),
And grandma drops us off at the airport.
We make it through security,
and you happily tell everyone we encounter,
"I'm going to the BEACH!"
They each smile and love your enthusiasm for life.
I do too.
We get on our first plane,
And arrive in Houston for a shorter layover than expected.
A large pack of cheez it's become our life support
As we begin a 2 hour flight that became 3.5 hours.
We finally arrive in Miami to find that the bus to South Beach is FREE!
It drops us a block from our place,
And I am underwhelmed seeing the exterior.
You are not phased in the slightest,
And burst through the front doors with your typical enthusiasm.

The elevator is barely big enough for us and the bag,
And doesn't even seem to be moving.
Somehow we make it to the top floor and exit.
"This smells like my cousins' house!"
Leaves your precious mouth as my mind immediately yells WEED.
I'll leave that for another day.
We open the door of our room,
And I contain my thoughts.
I am unimpressed.
You?
"Oh my goodness mom, I LOVE IT!"
I smile and promptly adopt your optimism with this place.
We throw our bags down and head out for dinner.
We decide to go downstairs to what feels like a gas station/cafe combo,
And order a pizza.
We wander around as it cooks,
And you decide on a Dr. Pepper before I spot a local IPA.
After the pizza is ready,
We head to the counter
And the cook who is now the cashier
Is stoked at my beer choice.
She speaks zero English but points to her hat and gives me a huge smile

Paired with an OK hand sign.
I made a friend AND a good beer choice!
We happily walk 3 minutes to the beach,
And have pizza by the starlight alone in the sand.
Your smile was illuminated by the stars
And we ran around the beach kicking up sand at each other and giggling.
Even though that would have served as the perfect ending to our first night,
It didn't end there.
We came back to the room
And I thought two big beds would be fun for us!
We each get our own full-sized bed
And can wave at each other.
You were upset that I didn't want to snuggle.
I decided to imagine what my 6 year old self would want in that moment.
My first thought?
A bed solely for jumping on!
I jumped out of bed and started jumping on yours.
I said let's have one bed to jump on,
And one bed for sleeping.
Your face lit up like your soul couldn't contain the joy anymore,
And you jumped with me.
We finished the night by watching the first half of Yes Day on Netflix

And my smile couldn’t be tamed.
That was even better than the best first night I could have imagined.

MUTE

Imagine a world on mute.
Sure, you get to skip some of the annoying noises
Like birds chirping at 4am as you are trying to sleep,
Dogs barking ceaselessly while attempting to watch a movie with your partner,
Horns honking in traffic because nobody seems to understand the concept of driving,
Babies crying just as you are trying to grab the last few groceries on your list.
But you also don't get to enjoy the perfect song after a long day of work
While submerged in a bubble bath.
Or experience a giggle escaping your child's mouth
After repeating the same joke for the hundredth time.
Or hearing those three little words escape the love of your life's mouth
Before falling asleep for the night.
I have always confided in music.
I am constantly tapped into what is playing around me.
I could be walking into Walmart
And immediately start singing every lyric.

Or I could be watching a movie
Where the scene is set in a coffee shop
And tune in to the indie song barely noticeable in the background.
Music is an audible way to express your soul.
Laughter really is the best medicine.
So the next time you get irritated at the person next to you incessantly clicking their pen,
Or your kids have asked if you are there yet for the 72nd time,
Just imagine not being able to hear anything at all.
My world would be a completely different place with no ability to turn up the volume.

TEETH

I keep having these horrific dreams
Where every single one of my teeth
Fall out at some point during the vision.
The latest one felt even more realistic
Than the hundreds I have had previously.
This is my most common recurring nightmare,
With the dream of being late on the first day of school
As a close second.
I was at school during the latest installment of tooth loss,
And I was at a campus that I often dream about but have never actually seen.
I was in a meeting with a handful of people
When I felt the first tooth slipping out.
Then the second,
Third,
And fourth
Promptly followed suit.
I turned around to slyly spit them into my hand
And place them carefully into my pocket
So none of them would slip out
For the world to see on the ground.
Then,
As the dream progresses,
every

last
one
of
my
teeth
fall
out.
The stress does seem to heat up in the dream
Around the teeth jumping away from the gums
that previously held them safely in place.
I wake up,
Exhausted yet again from another intense night
in my head,
And decide to look up some of the potential
meanings
Of this delightful dream.
Here are the related topics dealing with falling
teeth:
Anxiety about how you look to other people,
The inability to communicate properly,
Embarrassment in some aspect,
Poor diet,
"Money is on its way"
(Think tooth fairy money multiplied by every
tooth in your mouth
...Yes please),
Or you are going through a transitional period in
life.
Considering how many times

I have had these same visions over the years,
It is hard to pinpoint exactly what brings them on.
Definitely something to chew on.
…See what I did there?

Labels

I grew up with the label of being shy.
Thinking back,
I am not quite sure where that originally came from.
I was an only child for the first decade of my life,
So maybe I was actually just comfortable being by myself?
The word shy had to have been said around me.
About me.
I am not sure who
Or when.
Or where;
Or how the word was first used,
But I wouldn't have self-identified as shy.
I kept that label until college,
Or maybe even a few years after.
It didn't occur to me until my fifth or sixth country that I had traveled to
BY
MYSELF,
that this,
in fact,
Is not at all what a
"shy"
person

would
do.
One way flight to Vancouver for $100?
That was my first trip alone
And it was glorious.
Vancouver happened to be hosting the
International Jazz Festival
At the exact same time.
I wandered from place to place with nothing but
my journal,
A pen,
And my camera.
That was only the beginning.
Since then, I have been to
Italy,
Thailand,
Cambodia,
Vietnam,
New Zealand,
and Peru
ALL
BY
MYSELF.
And you know what?
I made friends.
Multiple human beings that I still keep in
contact with
From each of those adventures.
Is that what a shy person would do?

What other labels have we simply adopted
because we heard them so many times?
Make a list of words that you believe
define who you are.
Now look through that list
And really examine them
one
by
one.
Were any of those words stuck on you
without your consent?
It's time to revise and edit that list.
You get to be whoever you want to be.
Make
each
word
on
that
list
count.

Productive Procrastination

Productive Procrastination.
I can't be the only one that has a problem with this.
You know,
When you are supposed to be meeting that looming deadline,
But suddenly notice how dirty the floors are.
They must be swept and mopped immediately!
You miss the deadline,
But goodness check out how shiny and beautiful those floors look.
Or you have a meeting scheduled to begin in an hour,
Yet you realize your fingernails need trimming.
And while you have the clippers out,
Might as well cut your toenails too.
Then its two minutes prior to the start of the said meeting
And your hair is still in a messy bun on top of your head.
Yet even while staring at the disheveled mess on your head,
In the back of your mind,
You are praising yourself because your nails look fantastic.

Productive Procrastination.
Maybe this only happens to you once in a blue moon.
Or maybe this happens to you on the daily.
What is this productive procrastination trying to teach you?
Do you need to work on time management skills?
Or make daily to do lists to ensure everything gets done when it needs to?
Or, is this the universe's way of telling you that you are not on the right path?
Are you constantly putting work off?
Dust off the old resume and see what options are out there.
Do you wait to do the laundry until every last pair of panties is dirty
And you just can't delay any longer?
Talk to your partner or kids about making a list of duties around the house
That can be shared.
I know leaning into discomfort sounds counterintuitive,
But what if your productive procrastination is there to teach you something?
Just a thought.
Alright, I have to go do the dishes now.

GOALS

I get so darn emotional at the starting line of races now.
I was going to blame it on COVID,
But looking back,
That's not true.
My first full marathon was completed in December of 2019.
I had spent hours upon hours of my life training for that morning.
Not only do you need to be physically strong and prepared,
But you also have got to be mentally strong and prepared .
My second full marathon happened
Because I can't seem to say no when something is thrown at me
That I know will challenge and make me grow.
I was supposed to run a relay
With six other people
In December of 2020,
But we all know what was going on then.
Our entry was deferred to December of 2021.
I was the only person still ready and willing to run the relay,
So my theory was:
I will go pick up the shirts and bibs

So that I can run the first leg (7 miles)
Like I was supposed to,
And get the thrill of a race morning.
I arrived and asked the lady at the help desk
If there was any way I could change
The seven-person relay for the full marathon
Into a single entry for the half.
Cheaper fee, why not?
She kindly informed me that the half was full, but she would happily change me over to the marathon if I would like.
This is where I have approximately eight seconds to make a decision.
Is my body ready to run 26.2 miles in about 16 hours?
Nope.
BUT, I could run the first half
And then walk the rest.
The quick rationalization between the various parts of my brain
Resulted in the word yes coming out of my mouth.
My mouth caught on before my brain did,
And the next thing I know,
I have a single marathon bib printed out just for me.
Here goes nothing.
Marathon #1: I spent four months training specifically for.

Marathon #2: I began mentally preparing for the afternoon prior.
I should have known with the creation of my "run the first half, enjoy the second half" plan,
That it would fail immediately.
What can I say,
I get competitive.
My third marathon I signed up for six days in advance.
I realized I just need to get my body used to that length,
And then I may eventually be able to qualify for Boston.
I was having an in-depth conversation with a friend about our life goals for 2022 back in January.
I personally set my new year's goals in August,
As my new year has started during that month
Since I was a bright eyed and bushy tailed kindergartener.
My goals in August?
Qualify for the Boston Marathon (BQ in Runner-speak)
And meditate more.
I even got relatively intoxicated at a dinner with friends
And claimed my next running dream to be Boston
Back in July of 2021.

A dream is just a goal without a plan,
So I made a plan.
I signed up for what was advertised as
The fastest and flattest BQ race the next day.
But between July and April,
A lot could be accomplished,
Or avoided through procrastination.
Especially when you have a treadmill that is falling apart
After somehow surviving since the late 90's.
I finished my third marathon
ONE
MINUTE
AND
SEVENTEEN
SECONDS
TOO
SLOW
TO
QUALIFY.
I was pissed,
With absolutely no right to feel that way.
My body had just performed an amazing feat!
I was more than 25 minutes faster than my previous two.
Then, a few days later,
It occurred to me that on the next Boston Marathon race day,
I would be 35.

Which meant,
I needed a time under 3:35 to qualify.
I
DID
IT.
Have the dream.
Set the plan.
Meet your goals.
Hopefully, you will see me crying at the starting line of the Boston Marathon in 2023.

BIG LITTLE LESSONS

When Chloe was four,
She crashed her scooter in the living room below a mirror.
I quickly asked if she was okay
And told her to be careful.
She said it was an accident;
I said I know, but I need you to be careful.
She kept saying it was an accident,
And I kept saying but I need you to be careful,
until I walked away and went upstairs.
She slowly made her way up the staircase,
And entered the room where I was sitting, pouting,
She stated we need to talk about this.
I said okay, let's talk.
She awkwardly repeated it was an accident, barely moving her lips.
I calmly reiterated I understand that, but I was worried that you hurt yourself
Or broke the mirror,
And I need you to be careful.
Her response?
We have plenty of mirrors.
She ignored the larger part of my distress
because she saw something she could argue,
and chose to focus on that instead.

How often do we do this?
I know I am guilty of forgetting to apologize,
even when I know something is my fault,
Because I can focus on what could be construed
as someone else's fault.
We talked through the whole thing
again,
And each said we were sorry,
And that we loved each other the mostest.
We walked away from that small situation
as stronger individuals
And with a closer relationship than before.
Little lessons have a way
Of adding up to big lessons.

Dunkin'

You know when you walk into a room and you
can just feel the tension dripping from the
rafters?
It's uncomfortable.
It's unnerving.
It makes you want to slowly back away before
anyone notices you are there.
Maybe you are six and waltz into the middle of a
fight between your parents.
Or you are twelve and tip toe into a heated
conversation between your best friends.
Or maybe you are the one ranting as someone
else walks into the negative space you have
created.
Well, it happened again this weekend.
At Dunkin' Donuts.

Let's set the scene:
It's a beautiful, sunny Sunday.
The sky is lightly peppered with clouds.
The time is 11am.
A mother and her teenage daughter were
ordering and clearly on each other's very last
nerve.
The teen attempted to order a donut,
The mother promptly shut her down and said,

"No. We don't want that."
The teen just glared at her mother.
The mother met her gaze with her own icy version of it.
The mother ordered kolaches.
The teen said, no they won't want that.
The mother said she knew better and completed the order.
Arms were crossed.
Stances shifted.
Strangers silently checked in with each other through awkward eye contact.
Uncomfortable.
Unnerving.
I tried to offer a small smile to the teen, but her face reddened.
Embarrassment.
Even the faces of the workers were trying to refrain from showing their thoughts.
The mother moved to the far end of the counter to wait.
We ordered and attempted to add an ounce or two of cheer to the room.
No
Such
Luck.
Four minutes passed and the mother believed that was far too long to be subjected to the

waitlist at this establishment that was clearly beneath her.
She stormed back up to the counter
And berated a different worker than the poor soul from before.
One more minute and the bag was safely placed into the woman's hand.
She confidently walked out the door with her head held high,
As her daughter walked out with her eyes glued to the ground.
The energy in the room shifted immediately, and I began to wonder what made her act this way.
Was this typical?
Did she have a bad morning?
Did she have a rough childhood?
Is she now putting her daughter through the same yuck she went through?
Does she treat everyone this way?

Our job as a mom is to do better.
To be better.
To set a positive example.
To leave the world better than we found it.
The least we can do is treat everyone we meet with kindness.

You never know what kind of battle someone is facing, but it is important not to bring the war with you everywhere you go.

I mean, come on.
Who can be angry holding a donut with sprinkles on a sunny Sunday morning?

Starting Over

Starting over is such a daunting and difficult
task.
It can shake the foundation of who you are.
It can cause you to question the person you
were,
are,
And have the ability to someday become.
There are times when
I feel like I have a mental and emotional to do
list a mile long,
But reach for a beer or three instead.
Step one needs to be to learn to feel again.
Reconnect to the emotions bubbling up
in my innermost being
And becoming comfortable in owning and
displaying these emotions,
No matter who is looking.
On the outside,
I know I come off as a happy, energetic human,
even when I feel like I'm standing in the middle
of a crowded room,
Screaming my lungs out.
I refuse to let anyone steal my joy for even
one
more
minute.

I deserve more.
It is time that I return to the fundamentals of
who I am,
And begin exploring the deepest
needs,
wants,
And desires
That have been in me all along.

What's Next?

What's next?
This is a question people ask me
All of the time.
Whether they are talking about the next country
I am planning to explore,
Race I am going to run,
Or adventure Chloe and I will embark on.
The answer,
As of this very minute,
As I am sitting on my bed:
I have no idea.
There are so many more countries that I want to
experience.
I want to continue to race and challenge my
body as long as I have the ability to do so.
I want to watch Chloe's face light up with every
new experience we get to enjoy together.
I am 34 years old.
I have been to 32 countries.
I have run 57 half marathons.
I have run four full marathons.
I have been given the greatest dog and
companion I could possibly imagine.
I have carried a beautiful child in my belly,
and gotten to watch her blossom over the seven
years she has had on earth so far.

I have built wonderful relationships
With friends and family,
Both near and far.
I have found a profession that I absolutely love and have been blessed to be a part of for the past twelve years
In over five schools.
I have lived such an amazing life already,
And I do not take any of it for granted.
So, what's next?
I have no clue.
But I do know
That the Universe has never failed to amaze me, and I can't wait to see what is next.

www.ingramcontent.com/pod-product-compliance
Lightning Source LLC
Chambersburg PA
CBHW051735130826
49812CB00033B/867
9789357213530